Today is Market Day.

The farmers load their trucks with carrots and squashes, pears and mushrooms, fennel and chard.

We find our basket and make a list of the food we need.

The bakers warm their hands
as they unload cookies and
cakes, bread and scones.

We put on our coats
and scarves, then walk and run
and race down hill.

Today is Market Day.

We hear the bell ringing.

Everyone is gathering.

The whole town is here.

APPLES

Michael is here. We have waited all summer for his fresh, sweet apples. Michael sets out small and crisp Akane apples. He picked them yesterday in his orchard.

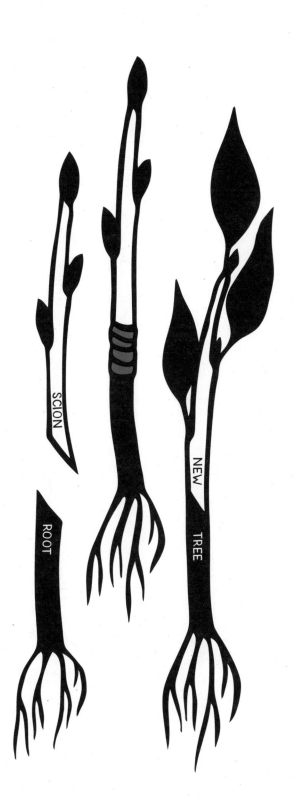

Michael tends four hundred apple trees. To plant his orchard, Michael traveled to old orchards and collected scions, small cuttings of branches, from the trees laden with the best fruit. He spliced each small scion to a rootstock (a small tree grown for its hardy roots). He then wrapped the scion and rootstock together with stretchy tape. This is called grafting. The scion wood grew into the rootstock's wood, and became a new tree, identical to one of the best trees in the old orchards. Michael's orchard is full of trees with history.

In winter, Michael prunes his trees to keep the branches from growing long and spindly. The trees need short, strong branches to hold heavy fruit. In summer, he pinches off some of the tiny developing apples. This allows the remaining apples to become big and round with all the nutrients the trees take up from the soil. In fall, the apples are ripe, and Michael reaches high to pick them for market.

Thank you, Michael, for these crisp new apples.

KALE

We wander through the market to see
what else is new this week. Colin and Genine
no longer have lettuce, but they do
have nice, dark green kale today.

Colin and Genine grow many kinds of kale on their farm. In the early days of spring, Genine plants the tiny, round kale seeds in trays of soil. The little plants grow first in the greenhouse, protected from the cold until they are big enough to be planted out in the field.

The field has rested all winter under a cover of rye grass. Rye grows quickly and its roots hold the soil in place so it does not wash away during the winter rains. In the spring, Colin tills the rye back into the earth with his tractor. Tiny beetles, worms, and bacteria underground eat the rye, breaking it up into food for the kale to use. The soil is dark and crumbly like chocolate cake, and makes the kale grow tender and delicious.

When the kale is stout and lovely, it is ready for harvest. Workers walk the rows snapping off leaves and making bunches. Genine gives each bunch a cleaning dunk in a deep tub of water. She places the kale, still dripping wet, into waxed boxes. Colin stacks the boxes in the farm's truck and drives to market. Today they have Dinosaur and Red Russian kale.

Thank you, Colin and Genine, for this sweet and happy kale.

SMOKED SALMON

Next on our market list is fish.

Steve is smiling this morning.

"Steve, what makes your smoked salmon so good?"

"Good fish. Rock salt. Alder smoke. Nothing else."

Steve smokes his salmon in an old smoker from a butcher shop that burned to the ground. The only thing left standing was the cast-iron smoker that had started the fire.

Steve buys his fish from local fishers, who catch the salmon with nets in the water and then deliver the fish fresh to Steve. He washes the salmon in a claw-foot tub and then filets them to remove the head, tail, fins, guts, and bones. He turns the scraps into compost for his vegetable garden.

To smoke the salmon, Steve soaks the fish in salt water for four days. The salt seeps in, drawing out the moisture and concentrating the rich fish oils. Steve then rinses the fish once more, and places the fillets skin-side up on racks in the smoker. He builds a gentle fire of alder wood at the bottom of the smoker. The fire releases natural sugars from the wood into the smoke, making the salmon taste smoky-sweet without adding sugar.

After two days, Steve opens the smoker and unloads the fish. The pieces are glistening and translucent red with charred markings from the wire trays. He wraps them up and takes them to market.

Thank you, Steve, for this good fish.

HONEY

Benjamin sells honey just across the aisle from Steve. Benjamin and Steve often trade fish for honey, honey for fish. Steve's favorite is maple honey. It is lightly colored and made from the flowers of bigleaf maple trees.

To make honey, bees collect nectar from flowers and take it to their hive. They fan the nectar with their wings to evaporate the moisture, turning the thin liquid into thick honey, food to last the winter. They make more honey than they need. It is this extra honey that Benjamin gathers.

Benjamin's beehives are wooden boxes filled with frames. The bees build wax honeycomb on the frames, and fill it with honey. To gather the honey, Benjamin puts on gloves, boots, a hat, and a big white suit. (Bees will sting dark objects that look like hungry bears.) Though he is protected from head to toe, Benjamin doesn't want to upset the bees, so he blows smoke into the hive with a tin smoker. The bees think there is a fire and begin to eat the honey to save it. Full of food, the bees become slow-moving and calm.

Benjamin carefully removes the frames from the hives. Buzzing fills the air. He cuts the wax caps off of the honeycomb and places the frames in an extractor that spins so fast that it spins the honey out. He pours the honey into jars to bring to market.

Thank you, Benjamin; thank you, bees; thank you, flowers, for this sweet honey.

BLUEBERRY TURNOVERS

At the bakery stand, Evan and Emma smile as
they take orders for bread, muffins, and macaroons.
We wait in line for blueberry turnovers. We love
the ones that have filling oozing out the sides.
Will there be some left when it is our turn?

At the bakery, Jessie and James make forty pounds of dough for turnovers. They mix flour with water and yeast, and knead the dough with a big mixing machine. The dough then rests so it can expand and grow.

Jessie weighs cold butter while James puts the dough through the sheeter, a machine that rolls it out thin. He carries the dough back to the table as if he were carrying a heavy, floppy baby. He grates the butter on top then folds the dough over and grates on more butter, then once again. Finally, he rolls it out and grates on even more butter. This will make the dough flaky when it bakes.

The dough needs a rest after all that work, as do the workers. The two bakers eat soft bread with fresh goat cheese.

Lunchtime is over! The bakers roll out the dough, covering the tabletop. They cut the dough into five-inch squares and put a scoop of goopy blueberry filling on each. They fold the squares over to form triangles and pinch the edges to seal them tight so no blueberry filling can ooze out (darn!). Early the next morning they bake the turnovers and bring them to market.

Thank you, Jessie and James, for this juicy, oozy blueberry turnover.

NAPKINS

We need a napkin! Let's go find Yukie. Yukie dyes fabric with indigo, using traditional Japanese methods. Indigo is a plant that turns cloth a rich blue, just right for wiping blueberry-stained faces.

Yukie has darkly stained tubs in her garage. Each holds water mixed with thirty pounds of dried indigo plant, which she orders from Japan.

Dark foam floats on top of the tubs. The indigo soup is alive with bacteria. The bacteria slowly feast on the indigo, releasing the blue color from the plant into the liquid of the tub. Cloth dipped in the dye will become blue. Yukie must stir the indigo soup twice a day and feed the hungry bacteria rice wine—"To keep them happy," she says.

Yukie has several ways of making images appear on dyed cloth. One way is called batik. She paints designs on the cloth with warm, melted wax. The wax cools and hardens. When the cloth is dipped in the dye, the areas painted with wax remain white. The wax is removed by melting it with a hot iron. Then Yukie's napkins and T-shirts are ready for market.

At market, Yukie keeps working. Her hands are always busy, sewing and drawing patterns onto white cloth for the next time she uses her indigo dye.

Thank you, Yukie, for these lovely blue napkins.

CHEESE

Market Day is cheese day as well.
We get our cheese from Heather and
her daughter, Katelyn. They let us taste
samples of the many cheeses that they make.

At the farm, the bleating of mama goats and their kids mixes with the calls of Heather's son, Zach, wondering where his mother is in the big barn. He wants to help feed the baby goats with bottles of fresh goat milk. The kids are kept separate from their mothers. Otherwise they would nurse all the time and there would be no milk to make cheese.

Zach also helps to lead the mother goats into the milking parlor. Heather's husband, Gary, attaches suction hoses to the goats' teats. The milking machine milks five goats at a time. After the milk is collected, the goats are led out and Zach leads in five more.

Heather pasteurizes the milk by heating it in a big tank. This kills any harmful bacteria. She adds vinegar to curdle the milk. She separates the solid curds from the liquid whey by straining the curds through cheesecloth. When the last bits of whey drip from the cheesecloth bundles, Heather has soft goat cheese.

Heather wraps small balls of cheese in oak leaves and takes them to market.

Thank you, Heather, Gary, Zach, Katelyn, and the mama and baby goats for this fresh cheese.

The band plays one last song and
the bell is rung. Market Day is done.

We walk home, taking turns carrying our
heavy basket full with food from the market.
The blueberry turnovers ride in our bellies.

The farmers and makers drive their nearly
empty trucks and vans back to their homes.

Tonight people all over town will eat well.

We remember all the people and all the creatures who worked to make this feast.

Thank you for this sustenance.

We will see you next Market Day.

CHEERS!

To farmers and makers everywhere and

especially those at the Olympia Farmers Market.

Thank you for your good work.

—N. M.

Artist's Note

I visit the Olympia Farmers Market every week. The food I gather there nourishes my family. It becomes a part of me. I was curious to find out how this food gets to market. I wanted to discover all the steps, all the tools and processes used to make the food that sustains my family. This book is that discovery.

Along the way, I also discovered who makes the food I eat. This was the most rewarding part of my research. I am thankful for all the work the farmers and makers do. Their skill, knowledge, and patience feed me. In particular, I thank Burnt Ridge Nursery, Kirsop Farm, Sea Blossom Seafoods, Pixie Honey, Blue Heron Bakery, Yukie Taylor, Twin Oaks Dairy, and Pigman's Organic Produce Patch. I wish I could have included everyone at the market. There are many more stories to share. I thank Anne Hull Seales, Anne de Marken, Scott Ogilvie, and Susan Van Metre for helping me share the story of my farmers market.

Every market is full of stories. Visit your local market and meet the people who make your food. Explore the source of the food that you eat. It will be a delicious journey!

The illustrations are cut paper. First, I draw the image on black paper, and then I cut it out with an X-Acto knife. I try to keep everything connected by a path of black paper. The paper becomes lacelike as the image emerges. I decide the width of line and what will be black or white as I cut. There is no erasing, so if I make a mistake, I just have to keep cutting and find a solution. The cut paper is then scanned, and color is added digitally.

Cataloging-in-Publication Data has been applied for and may be
obtained from the Library of Congress.
ISBN 978-0-8109-9738-7

Text and illustrations copyright © 2011 Nikki McClure
Book design by Chad W. Beckerman

Printed and bound in U.S.A.
10 9 8 7 6 5 4 3 2 1

ABRAMS
THE ART OF BOOKS SINCE 1949
115 West 18th Street
New York, NY 10011
www.abramsbooks.com